ANIMALS IN THE WILD

JAPANESE MACAQUE

Annette Whipple

A Crabtree Forest Book

Crabtree Publishing
crabtreebooks.com

Notes for Readers and Class Discussion

This book is designed to teach readers about core subject areas, build curiosity, and inspire further investigation. Readers are encouraged to build upon what they already know about the subject and engage in topics they want to learn more about. Here are a few guiding questions to prompt reflection and discussion. Possible answers appear in red.

Before Reading:

Read the title and look at the table of contents. What do you already know about Japanese macaques?

- *I know that Japanese macaques live in large groups called troops.*
- *I know that Japanese macaques are also called snow monkeys.*

What would you like to learn about Japanese macaques?

- *I would like to learn about what the Japanese macaque eats.*
- *I would like to learn whether the Japanese macaque has any predators.*

During Reading:

Pause after reading each page or chapter. What questions do you have about what you read? What are you curious to know?

- *I wonder why Japanese macaques are matrilineal animals.*
- *I am curious to know why Japanese macaques spend a large part of their day grooming.*

Make connections to what you are reading. How is this like something you already know?

- *I know that some animals, such as elephants, live in groups led by females.*
- *I know that one of the biggest threats to many animals is habitat loss due to human actions, leaving them with fewer places to live and find food.*

After Reading:

Recall key details about the book. What was the author trying to teach readers?

- *The author was trying to teach readers about the characteristics, behaviors, and habitats of Japanese macaques.*
- *The author was trying to teach readers that Japanese macaques are important to their habitat for many reasons, including seed dispersal.*

How did the images and captions help you understand more?

- *The photographs helped to show me how Japanese macaques live together and communicate with each other.*
- *The captions helped me understand new details about Japanese macaques.*

Table of Contents

Introduction
Meet the Japanese Macaque 4

Chapter 1
What Do They Look Like? 6

Chapter 2
Home and Habitat 12

Chapter 3
What to Eat? 18

Chapter 4
Japanese Macaque Behavior 24

Chapter 5
The Next Generation 32

Chapter 6
Japanese Macaque Conservation.............. 38

Glossary 44
Index 46
Comprehension Questions 47
About the Author 48

Meet the Japanese Macaque

What furry animal with a pink face is known for hanging around in **hot springs**? It's the Japanese macaque! This Asian **primate** is also known for its intelligence and sense of fun.

Japanese macaques are also called snow monkeys because they live in the north of Japan where snow is common. They live farther north than other primates.

Mah-KAK

Macaque is pronounced mah-KAK. The Japanese macaque is just one of 23 different **species** of macaques in the world. They are considered Old World monkeys—part of the largest primate family. Old World monkeys are **native** to Africa and Asia. The Japanese macaque, or *Nihonzaru*, is native to Japan.

Mammals

Japanese macaques are mammals. All mammals share some of the same characteristics. They keep a constant body temperature even as their environment gets warmer or colder. Hair or fur covers their skin. Females give birth to live young and feed their young with the milk the mother produces.

Nihon means Japan in the Japanese language. *Zaru*, pronounced "saru," means monkey.

Chapter 1

What Do They Look Like?

Japanese macaques have distinct pink to ruby-red faces. Their rumps are also this bright color. Like other monkeys, Japanese macaques have tails. Their stumpy tails are only around 3.5 inches (9 cm) long.

As Big as a Backpack

Japanese macaques are a bit taller than a large backpack. Males average about 22 inches (56 cm) tall and about 25 pounds (11 kg). Females are a bit smaller. They're about 21 inches (53 cm) tall and weigh about 19 pounds (9 kg).

Dimorphism

Adult male and female Japanese macaques differ in size, appearance, strength, and weight. These differences are called sexual dimorphism. Sexual dimorphism is easily seen differences between sexes—beyond their different reproductive organs. They are common in many animals, including humans.

Body Hair

Brown, yellow-brown, or gray fur covers the bodies of Japanese macaques. This fur changes with the seasons. It thickens as temperatures get colder. This helps Japanese macaques survive harsh winters with temperatures below 0 °Fahrenheit (–18 °C).

A Japanese macaque's fur is shaggy, and brown to gray in color.

Winter and Summer Coats

The Japanese macaque's thick fur works as a kind of **insulation**. In fall, its coat grows thicker to help it retain body heat in cold winters. As temperatures warm in the spring, the Japanese macaque's fur thins and sheds.

Most Old World monkeys such as macaques have opposable thumbs. The exception is colobus monkeys, who do not have thumbs.

Thumbs-Up (Or Down)

Primates are a group of mammals with large brains. They typically have flat fingernails instead of hooves or claws. Some primates, including apes, humans, and many monkeys, have opposable thumbs. This means their thumbs can move without moving the other fingers. They easily move things in their hands with their thumbs.

Trees are "safe places" for Japanese macaques. Their incredible upper-body strength means they can easily climb trees to escape **predators**. Trees also provide shade in hot summers.

Monkey Walk

Typically, Japanese macaques walk like other monkeys—on all four limbs. However, they can also walk more upright on just their back legs. They do this when they need to carry something in both hands. Like many monkeys, Japanese macaques are well-suited for living in trees and walking on land.

Chapter 2

Home and Habitat

Japanese macaques are native to the island country of Japan, which is part of the continent of Asia.

Northern Monkey

Japanese macaques inhabit some of Japan's smaller islands as well as three of its four main islands: Honshu, Shikoku, and Kyushu. They live farther north than any other monkey, which is why they're also known as snow monkeys.

Deciduous Forest Dwellers

Japanese macaques dwell, or live, in two main ranges, or areas. In the northern range, the year-round temperatures average a cool 52 °Fahrenheit (11 °C). Here, they live in deciduous forests where the trees lose their leaves in the fall and regrow them in the spring.

People from around the world visit Joshinetsu-Kogen National Park to watch Japanese macaques bathe in the hot springs.

Hot Tub Monkeys

The winters are harsh in the northern range. Snow can be 3 feet (1 m) deep. Japanese macaques bathe themselves in the warm waters of Joshinetsu-Kogen National Park, also known as Snow Monkey Park, to warm themselves in the winter. These hot springs are heated by nearby volcanoes.

Evergreen Forest Dwellers

In the southern range, the Japanese macaque **habitat** is warm and rainy. The year-round average temperature is 68 °Fahrenheit (20 °C). In this range, Japanese macaques live in evergreen forests where the trees don't drop their leaves according to the season. Instead, the forests remain green year round. The southern range may be warmer than the northern range, but winters are still cold and unpleasant.

In the winter, Japanese macaques move to lower **elevations**. The weather is still cold there, but it's not as severe.

Cheeky Monkeys

In the 1950s, Japanese **primatologists** began to study a **troop** of free-roaming Japanese macaques. They used food so they could get near them to study their behavior. The troop was located in Arashiyama near the ancient city of Kyoto on the island of Honshu. By 1972, these monkeys, called the Arashiyama group, had grown used to being fed. Their population exploded into two groups. They started to overrun their territory.

The Arashiyama group became unafraid of humans—which was dangerous for both the monkeys and humans. They stole food from gardens and began sleeping and pooping in Buddhist temples.

Moving On

In order to protect the 150 Japanese macaques, the primatologists decided they needed to move some to an enclosed ranch in Texas in the United States. The Texas environment was new to the macaques—especially the weather and wildlife. At first, some macaques died. But they soon learned to survive and thrive, or do well. The animals **foraged** for foods new to them, including mesquite beans and cactus fruits. They also learned to avoid being **prey** to animals such as coyotes, eagles, and rattlesnakes.

Around 120 Japanese macaques now live at the Iwatayama Monkey Park in Arashiyama, while between 400 and 600 live at the Born Free USA Primate Sanctuary in Texas.

Chapter 3

What to Eat?

As omnivores, Japanese macaques eat both plants and animals. They mainly consume fruits, leaves, and fallen seeds. But their diet includes more than 200 kinds of plants.

A Side of Bird Eggs

These monkeys also eat insects and bird eggs, as well as small critters such as snails and crayfish. Japanese macaques store food in their cheek pouches.

Seasonal Eaters

What Japanese macaques eat depends on the season. During summer and early fall they eat mostly fruits and some seeds. They depend on leaves in the winter as well as nuts they have stored. In the spring they eat flowers and young leaves.

Meal Times

Japanese macaques don't forage all day. Instead, they eat on a schedule. In warmer weather they'll eat just two to three times each day. In the winter they add another meal to the schedule and eat up to four times a day.

Leafy Diet

Leaves make up much of what they eat. These monkeys prefer to forage on the ground, but they also climb trees to get leaves to eat. When they do this, they accidentally help sika deer who live in the same habitat. These deer compete with the Japanese macaques for food. As the macaques forage at the tops of trees, leaves fall to the ground. Then the sika deer eat the fallen leaves, which they wouldn't have been able to reach on their own.

Sika deer are also called northern spotted deer or Japanese deer. They live in forests in Japan.

Wildlife biologists often study animal **scat** to determine the health of an animal and where its food sources are located.

Spreading Seeds

Japanese macaques help their habitat in another way—without even trying! They are an important **seed disperser**. Japanese macaques eat a lot of fruits and seeds. About one-third of the seeds they eat pass through their **digestive systems** and back into the environment.

As Japanese macaques move through their habitat, they leave scat—with seeds intact—where they wander. The seeds spread throughout the forest and grow into new plants. This is a natural process of seed dispersal which helps forests grow and thrive.

Chapter 4

Japanese Macaque Behavior

Japanese macaques are **matrilineal** animals. Troops of both males and females are led by females. Troops can include hundreds of members, all organized by **dominant** females.

Social Rankings

Each monkey in a troop has a social **ranking**. Those with higher rankings have more **privileges** and are considered more important than those with lower rankings. Each female Japanese macaque inherits her mother's social rank.

Troops of macaques include both females and males. Males sometimes split off into their own groups.

Female Leadership and Alphas

Males within a troop also have social rankings. The most dominant male is called the alpha. An alpha male is the leader of the males in the troop. The alpha keeps this position through a strong relationship with the dominant females. They have the power to determine his role.

Social Animals

Japanese macaques are social animals. In the wild, they often live in troops of 20 to 50 macaques of all ages and sexes. Some troops number in the hundreds. The size of the troop is usually based on food availability. Troops include more females than males.

Social Grooming

Macaques spend a large part of their days grooming, or cleaning, other macaques in the troop. Grooming builds and maintains social relationships. Grooming is also **kinship** related. Females groom other females who they are related to matrilineally. Mothers pass their grooming skills on to their offspring.

Vocal Communication

Japanese macaques communicate with sounds called vocalizations, as well as through body language. They interact with macaques in their own troops as well as others. Vocalizations let others know how they feel. Typically, their sounds are peaceful and soothing. They also have defensive and warning sounds. When threatened, they holler to warn their group of danger. When traveling, they use their voices to keep the troop together.

Body Language

Communication isn't just through sounds. They use body language as well. Their facial expressions change to show mood. Japanese macaques change their posture too, often displaying their posteriors, or behinds, to signal **submissiveness** to another more dominant macaque. They also show their posteriors when ready to **mate**.

These intelligent animals pass learned behavior on from **generation** to generation.

Day Monkeys

Japanese macaques are diurnal, which means they are most active during the day. That's when they travel, feed, and groom one another. Days also provide plenty of time for rest. At night, Japanese macaques typically sleep in trees. They also sleep on the ground near rocks or fallen trees. In wintry weather they huddle together for warmth while they sleep.

Japanese macaques live, climb, and leap among the trees.

Ground and Water

Japanese macaques are good swimmers and often gather together to swim, as well as sit in warm waters. These monkeys also spend quite a bit of time on the ground—with males spending more time on the ground than females.

Chapter 5

The Next Generation

The **breeding** season of Japanese macaques is from March to September. They're **polygamous**, so males and females both have multiple partners in a season.

Ladies' Choice

Typically, the female chooses a male. She considers his rank in the troop as well as how long he has been with the group. However, alpha males are not always the ones female macaques prefer to mate with. They may choose to mate with males of any rank. They may also mate with several males in a season.

Sometimes male Japanese macaques may wander off to mate with females in a different troop.

Courtship

The mating process involves a period of courtship, where the male and female spend a few days together. Courtship is important for Japanese macaques. The male and female bond by feeding, nesting, and traveling together before mating.

Pregnancy and Birth

The female Japanese macaque is pregnant for about five and a half months. The female prefers to be alone when she is ready to give birth. She looks for a safe and quiet place on the ground and remains close to the group yet set apart.

Japanese macaques usually give birth to one infant at a time. They raise their babies for about a year and a half before having another.

Baby Macaques

At birth, the average Japanese macaque weighs just 1.2 pounds (540 g). This is about the weight of a bottle of water. Its body is covered in dark-brown hair. At first, the mother stays apart from the rest of the troop while she cares for and nurses her infant.

Mothers raise newborns on their own, but stay very close to their troops.

First Weeks

For the first four weeks, a mother carries her infant on her belly. The baby drinks its mother's milk. By three to four months of age, the young macaque is fully mobile, or able to move around on its own. It begins **weaning** around six to eight months of age, although the process takes much longer. The mother continues to carry her offspring on her back even after one year of age.

Most females reproduce until about age 25, and typically live to be a bit older.

Troop for Life!

Females remain in the same family troop for life. Once mature, males leave their natal, or birth, troop. They spend the rest of their lives in different troops. They may live alone at times before joining all-male troops. As females choose mates, the availability of males from different troops increases the **genetic diversity** of the species.

Chapter 6

Japanese Macaque Conservation

Japanese macaques are small animals, but they don't have many predators. Birds such as mountain hawk-eagles hunt macaques. They are also prey to Japanese wolves and foxlike raccoon dogs. But humans are the biggest threat to Japanese macaques.

Habitat Loss

Japanese macaques have lost much of their habitat to historical **deforestation**. During the 1800s and throughout the 1900s, people cut down forests for logging, agriculture, and housing. Forests were cleared to make room for animal grazing. Japan grew rapidly over the later half of the 1900s, with new roads and building construction contributing to deforestation.

Japanese macaques were displaced, or forced out of the areas where they lived, by the expansion of **urban** areas into their habitat.

Farmers consider Japanese macaques agricultural pests. Some have been killed by farmers protecting crops.

Macaques vs. Humans

With more people living in and near their territory, Japanese macaques don't fear humans as they once did. Increased exposure to humans means more conflicts. Macaques raid and damage crops and property. Both macaques and humans have become more aggressive in their contact with each other. In 2022, Japanese macaques attacked and injured at least 45 people in Yamaguchi City on the island of Honshu. Some of the monkeys broke into homes. The macaques had to be subdued with tranquilizer guns and traps.

Macaque Future

Japanese macaques have existed in Japan for 430,000 years. They thrived for thousands of them. Hunting and the destruction of forest habitat meant that by the 1950s, their population numbered only a few dozen. **Conservation** efforts in the following decades led to a population boom. By the late 1970s, more than 2,000 Japanese macaques were culled, or killed, annually to keep the population managed.

Animal conservationists say urban expansion in the last 40 years has led to increased competition for space and more human–macaque conflict in Japan.

Delicate Balance

Currently, scientists do not consider Japanese macaques to be vulnerable or **endangered** based on the threats they face for survival. Although not immediately threatened, the government protects them. Today most Japanese macaques live on reserves which have been set aside for them. Many macaques on the reserves rely on humans to provide additional food during winters because of limited food sources within the reserves.

Although the population is currently stable, Japanese macaques continue to face threats of hunting, deforestation, and food scarcity.

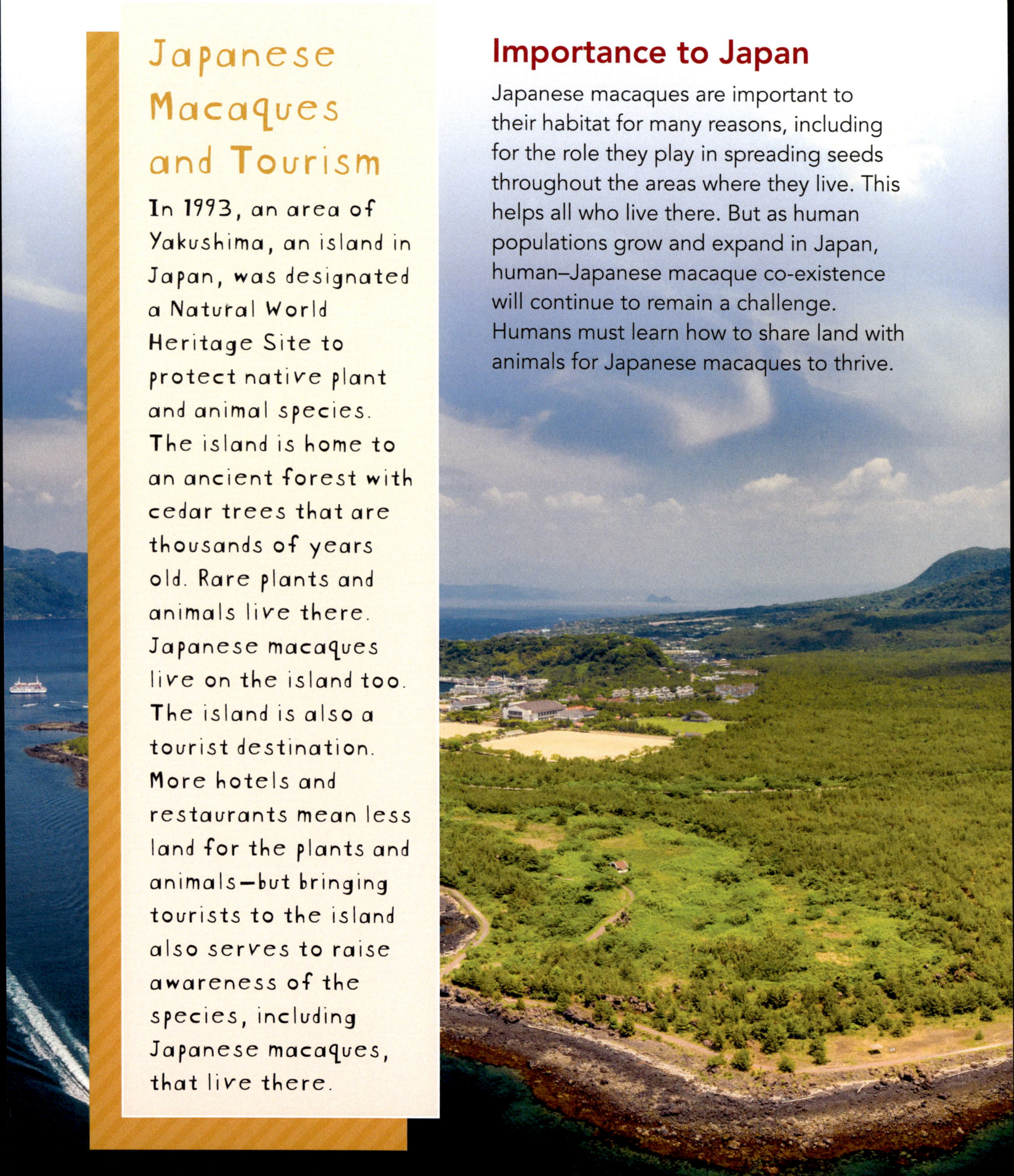

Japanese Macaques and Tourism

In 1993, an area of Yakushima, an island in Japan, was designated a Natural World Heritage Site to protect native plant and animal species. The island is home to an ancient forest with cedar trees that are thousands of years old. Rare plants and animals live there. Japanese macaques live on the island too. The island is also a tourist destination. More hotels and restaurants mean less land for the plants and animals—but bringing tourists to the island also serves to raise awareness of the species, including Japanese macaques, that live there.

Importance to Japan

Japanese macaques are important to their habitat for many reasons, including for the role they play in spreading seeds throughout the areas where they live. This helps all who live there. But as human populations grow and expand in Japan, human–Japanese macaque co-existence will continue to remain a challenge. Humans must learn how to share land with animals for Japanese macaques to thrive.

Yakushima is home to roughly 16 mammal species, 150 bird species, and 1,900 plant species.

breed (breed): To produce offspring

conservation (kon-ser-VEY-shuhn): The protection of animals, plants, and their habitats

deforestation (dee-fawr-uh-STEY-shuhn): The permanent clearing of forests or large areas of trees

digestive system (dahy-JES-tiv SIS-tuhm): The set of organs in the body, including the stomach and intestines, that turns food into energy and nutrients

dominant (DOM-uh-nuhnt): Being the most important or most powerful

elevation (el-uh-VEY-shuhn): The height of a place, usually measured above or below sea level

endangered (en-DEYN-jerd): An animal or plant species that is considered to be at a very high risk of becoming extinct in the wild

forage (FAWR-ij): To search for food

generation (jen-uh-REY-shuhn): The period of time between the birth of parents and the birth of their offspring

genetic diversity (juh-NET-ik dahy-VUR-si-tee): The range of different inherited traits within a species

habitat (HAB-i-tat): The place where an animal or plant naturally lives and grows

hot spring (hot spring): A source of hot water that flows naturally from the ground

insulation (in-suh-LEY-shuhn): Something that protects from cold or heat

kinship (KIN-ship): The relationship between members of a family

mate (meyt): When a male and female animal join together for the purpose of producing offspring

matrilineal (ma-truh-LIN-ee-uhl): Refers to tracing descent through the mothers in a family

native (NEY-tiv): Something that lives or grows naturally in a place

polygamous (puh-LIG-uh-muhs): Having more than one mate at a time

predator (PRED-uh-ter): An animal that hunts other animals for food

prey (prey): An animal that is hunted by other animals as food

primate (PRAHY-meyt): A type of mammal that includes people, apes, and monkeys

primatologist (prahy-muh-TAHL-uhj-ist): A scientist who studies primates

privilege (PRIV-uh-lij): A benefit that is given only to certain individuals

ranking (RANG-king): Position or status within a group

scat (skat): Animal droppings, or poop

seed disperser (seed dih-SPURS-ur): Something in nature, such as an animal, water, or wind, that moves seeds away from the parent plant to a new place where they can grow

species (SPEE-sheez): A group of living things that are very similar and can have babies together

submissiveness (suhb-MIS-iv-nes): A willingness to obey or be controlled by another

troop (troop): A name for certain groups of animals or people

urban (UR-buhn): Of or having to do with cities

wean (ween): To start feeding a young animal food other than its mother's milk

INDEX

conflict with humans 16, 39, 40, 42
conservation 40–42

deforestation 38, 41
digestive systems 23

endangered species 41

foraging 17, 20, 21
forests 13, 15, 21, 23, 38, 40, 42
fur/hair 4, 5, 8–9, 35

grooming 27, 30

Honshu 13, 16, 39
hot springs 4, 14

infants 34–36

Japan 5, 12, 13, 21, 38, 40, 42
Joshinetsu-Kogen National Park 14

mating 29, 32–33, 37

Old World monkeys 5, 10
omnivores 18

predators 11, 38
prey 17, 38
primates 4, 5, 10, 17

reserves 41

scat 23
seeds 18, 19, 23, 42
sika deer 21
size 6–7, 35
snow monkeys 5, 13, 14
social rank 24, 25, 32

tails 6
territories 16, 39
Texas 17
thumbs 10
tourism 42
troops 16, 24–28, 32, 33, 35, 37

urban expansion 38, 40

vocalization 28

Yakushima 42–43

COMPREHENSION QUESTIONS

1. True or False: Japanese macaques are solitary animals that prefer to spend their days by themselves.

2. Japanese macaques play an important role in their environment because they help to disperse ___________.

   a. insects
   b. fruit
   c. seeds

3. Japanese macaques are ___________.

   a. herbivores
   b. omnivores
   c. carnivores

4. True or False: Japanese macaques are good swimmers.

5. A large part of a Japanese macaque's day is spent ______.

   a. grooming other macaques
   b. fighting other macaques
   c. sleeping

6. True or False: Troops of Japanese macaques are usually led by males.

7. Japanese macaques are also called _______ monkeys.

   a. red-faced
   b. snow
   c. short-tailed

8. True or False: The Japanese macaque is an endangered species.

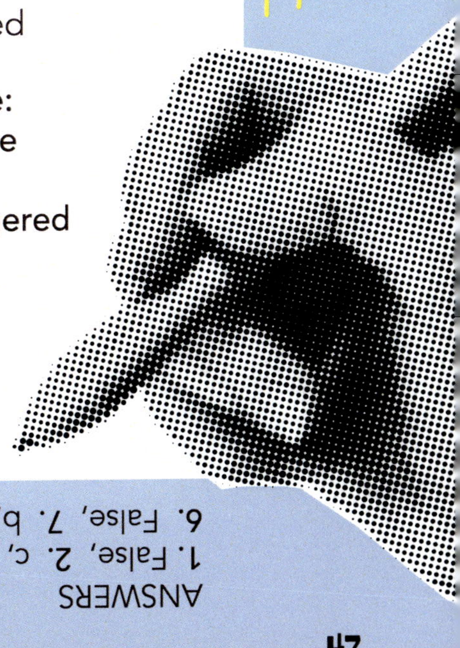

ANSWERS
1. False, 2. c, 3. b, 4. True, 5. a,
6. False, 7. b, 8. False

About the Author

Annette Whipple is the author of many children's books, including *The Laura Ingalls Wilder Companion: A Chapter-by-Chapter Guide, Whooo Knew? The Truth About Owls, and Quirky Critter Devotions: 52 Wild Wonders for Kids.* When Annette's not reading or writing, you might find her baking for her family in Pennsylvania. Get to know her at AnnetteWhipple.com.

Written by: Annette Whipple

Editor: Ellen Rodger

Proofreader: Melissa Boyce

Design and layout: Tammy McGarr

Production manager: Candice Campbell

Image Credits

Shutterstock: K I Photography p 6 (left), STUDIO BONOBO TOSHIO S p 14 (top), Cristi Croitoru p 16

Wikimedia Commons: Creative Commons p 17 (bottom), p 43 (bottom), (top right)

All other images from Shutterstock

Crabtree Publishing

crabtreebooks.com **800-387-7650**

Hardcover 978-1-0398-7481-7
Paperback 978-1-0398-8435-9
Ebook (pdf) 978-1-0398-8194-5
Epub 978-1-0398-8314-7

Published in Canada
Crabtree Publishing
616 Welland Avenue
St. Catharines, Ontario
L2M 5V6

Published in the United States
Crabtree Publishing
347 Fifth Avenue
Suite 1402-145
New York, New York, 10016

Library and Archives Canada Cataloguing in Publication
Available at Library and Archives Canada

Library of Congress Cataloging-in-Publication Data
Available at the Library of Congress

Printed in the U.S.A./CP022026